Dear David and Cathy,
There is nothing too
hard for the Lord
Smith

"Can a woman forget her nursing child, that she should not have compassion on the son of her womb? yea, they may forget, yet will I not forget you."

- God
(Isaiah 49:15)

Published by Love Without Reason®, Inc, Chattanooga, TN 37424

Printed in India
First Printing, 2012

ISBN 978-0-615-73580-1

Love Without Reason®
P.O. Box 21009, Chattanooga, TN 37424
www.lovewithoutreason.org

Concepts and ideas by David Simon
Photograph of Philip Mathews by Lovely Mathai
Compiled, edited and designed by Santhosh Mathews

Ordering Information:
Quantity sales: Special discounts are available on quantity purchases by corporations, associations, orders by U.S. trade bookstores and wholesalers and others please contact the publisher at the address above or email the publisher at info@lovewithoutreason.org.

A Mother's

Heart

SUSAN MATHEWS

Acknowledgement

I would first give all glory and praise to God for demonstrating to me His own love without reason. Let His name be exalted and may all draw near to Him.

To David Simon, my "little" brother, I'm thankful for your direction, guidance and creativity to open our eyes to see the book in front of us. God bless you.

I would not have had the time to write this book without the help of both sets of parents and their willingness and sacrifice in babysitting, cooking and cleaning. God bless you Mom, Dad, Pappa and Mummy.

My three little munchkins, I love you so much. Thank you for being patient with me. Lastly, as the Word says, the last will be first, and the first will be last. To my husband, Santhosh, thank you for your love, your kindness and generosity to me. May grace lead us home!

Introduction

A mother's heart would naturally start at the time of motherhood; therefore my story begins when we discovered we were expecting our first child. At the time of our five month ultrasound, in March of 2000, many birth defects were discovered. The initial report was that there was no hope that my baby would live. No hope.

My Testimony

I thank God because He takes our hopeless situations and transforms them into situations full of hope. The life threatening issue was the absent stomach on our first ultrasound. Our doctor felt that our baby's stomach was probably trapped in the lung cavity which would not allow the lungs to function properly at birth.

The craniofacial defects and heart defects along with the missing stomach led our specialist to the thought that the best medical option was an abortion. We returned home with a heavy heart. Our Pastor, V.P. Abraham came to pray with us and encouraged us in the faith and gave us a Word from God found in Jeremiah 18: 3, 4

"So I went to the potter's house, and sure enough, the potter was there, working away at his wheel. Whenever the pot the potter was working on turned out badly, as sometimes happens when you are working with clay, the potter would simply start over and use the same clay to make another pot." [MSG]

The potter mentioned in that passage was forming a vessel, which was marred in his hand. Yet, the potter did not throw away the clay, instead refashioned the clay to another vessel. We believed that God was refashioning our baby in the womb. Isn't He the Creator who fashioned the world out of nothing? In the same way, He fashions you and me, forming us into the people we are called to be. This was the beginning of miracles!

Philip Mathews was born alive on July 27th of 2000, by the grace of God. He is a witness to the fact that God hears and answers prayers.

This is a piece of my heart and a little more of the journey over the past twelve years since our first child, Philip, was born. I share with you the joys, the struggles, the pain, and most importantly the life-changing love and power of my Heavenly Father. That love, is beyond reason. That love picked me up out the miry clay and set my feet on a Rock, where I will not be moved.

Our experiences with Philip helped us form Love Without Reason® in 2007 whose mission is to fight the evils of sex trafficking and help people like Philip born with facial deformities.

For you created my inmost being; you knit me together in my mother's womb.

I praise you because I am fearfully and wonderfully made; your works are wonderful, I know that full well.

My frame was not hidden from you when I was made in the secret place, when I was woven together in the depths of the earth.

Your eyes saw my unformed body; all the days ordained for me were written in your book before one of them came to be.

How precious to me are your thoughts God!
How vast is the sum of them!

Were I to count them, they would outnumber the grains of sand — when I awake, I am still with you.

- ***Psalm139: 13-18***

Happy Anniversary

July 17th marked another year of married life. It is so hard to believe that Santhosh and I have been married for fifteen years. So I took a few minutes to think about the last fifteen years of life. Here are a few thoughts:

If someone had told me fifteen years ago that I would be so passionate about children born with birth defects or children who were victims of trafficking, that I would form a nonprofit organization to rescue them, I think I would've laughed. "Who? Me?" My thought was to get married, raise a family, be a nurse, go to church, take care of parents and live happily ever after.

Then came Philip. He turned my "perfect" world upside down. And I would do it all over again. I get shaken sometimes when I think that there was a chance that he would never have been born alive. God is so faithful, in spite of my lack of faith.

Though the years have been hard with struggles and worries about Philip's healthcare needs, he always had the most excellent health care. Every child deserves refuge, hope, and love. Not one child deserves to be reproached or discarded to live a life of shame. I pray that Love Without Reason® would bring the refuge, hope, and love that all children deserve. Please pray that God would lead us in this endeavor!

Philip's Faith

Our church, Chattanooga Christian Assembly, hosted former Bollywood singer/songwriter Mr. Vijay Benedict and his family for a concert and a time of sharing their testimony of accepting Christ as their Savior. The concert was awesome and the testimony very touching. Later that evening Mr. Benedict and family gathered for dinner at my parent's house. Mrs. Benedict saw the "before" pictures of Philip that my parents had placed on the dining room table and called Philip to sit with her. She told Philip that he should pray every day that God would heal him and make his face symmetrical so that both sides of his face look the same. He was patient and listened to all that the dear sister said.

Then Philip responded and shook his head emphatically, "I do pray that God would heal me, but sometimes God tells me I have to wait." I wept as I heard his response. What faith the child has, and what faith does his mother have?

I know and believe that a day is coming where Philip will not run into anyone or anything due to the lack of vision on the right side of his face. I know and believe a day is coming where I will not have to see him cock his head so that his functioning ear is turned to hear someone talking to him. What about his curved spine? I know that God could just say the word and his spine would be straight! I have been praying for this and what's taking so long? It's so hard to wait!!

And that evening I believe God was also reminding me, every prayer has been heard, every tear has been seen, but I have to wait. Wait on the Lord's time.

"Wait on the LORD: be of good courage, and he shall strengthen your heart: wait, I say, on the LORD."

- ***Psalm 27:14***

Let Not Your Heart Be Troubled

Before each of Philip's surgeries, we teach him a Bible verse. For instance in 2005 with his jaw surgery, he learned Hebrews 13:5 *"I will never leave you, nor forsake you."* I still remember telling Philip that Pappa and I could not be with him during the surgery, but what did Jesus say? And he responded, "I will never leave you, nor forsake you." Those were the words he said as he left our arms and went to the operating room.

After his ear surgery in January 2008, he was quoting Joshua 1:9 *"Be strong and 'have a good courage' for the Lord your God is with you!"* He even shared it with his nurse, as she was pulling out his intravenous line.

Before his nasopharyngeal flap repair in August 2008, we taught him John 14:1 *"Let not your heart be troubled, ye believe in God, believe also in me."* After surgery, the surgeon called us and told us that Philip's airway had closed once the breathing tube had been removed. Our surgeon and anesthesiologist felt it would be better to re-insert the breathing tube and keep him on the ventilator. Philip went straight into the intensive care unit.

Though Philip has always had some trouble coming out of anesthesia (due to his abnormal and small airway) he did not have trouble with the last two surgeries. We had hoped this was due to his growth and the enlarging of his airway. The surgeon felt that the difficulty with his breathing may partly be due to his airway size, the flap surgery, the anesthesia and his small jaw size. All of it combined contributed to the obstruction of his airway. The hope is that with time, medicines to reduce swelling, and rest as he remains on the ventilator over the weekend, the doctor will be ready to remove the breathing tube on Monday.

I went through shock, I guess. It was almost like a dream or nightmare. This was supposed to be a simple one hour procedure, two or three day recovery, and go home. I was reminded, "Let not your heart be troubled, believe in God, believe also in me."

How Long, Lord? How Long?

I think I've been in a kind of spiritual slump. Frustrations, unanswered prayers, questions, doubts… Pretty much what David says in Psalms 13: 1-4 [KJV]

"How long wilt thou forget me, O LORD? For ever? How long wilt thou hide thy face from me?

How long shall I take counsel in my soul, having sorrow in my heart daily? How long shall mine enemy be exalted over me?

Consider and hear me, O LORD my God: lighten mine eyes, lest I sleep the sleep of death;

Lest mine enemy say, I have prevailed against him; and those that trouble me rejoice when I am moved."

Since Philip's discharge from the hospital, he has had a horrible time with his breathing when he sleeps at night. He struggles with each breath, and we have struggled in watching him and not knowing what to do to help him. We change positions, sleep with him in the rocking chair, everything we know to do. We discussed his breathing with his doctor on Friday. They have been monitoring his oxygen level at night while he slept for the last 2 nights. His oxygen levels range from

78% to 100% (normal above 92%). I've just felt so helpless. I didn't know what to do, how to help. He is so tired, because he is not getting to sleep at night. How long can this go on? How many tears before there is an answer?

Our church family gathered together around Philip to pray for him on Sunday morning. Though I hoped for a change on Sunday night, his condition did not change.

I do not know the answer to Philip's breathing struggles. I do not know how long he will have to breathe like this. But ONE thing I know:

Philip has a call on his life. God reminded me of this again with the verse in Psalms 118:17 shortly after his recent flap surgery, *"I shall not die, but live, and declare the works of the Lord."* I know my God has seen every tear, heard every prayer, and listened to each cry. Weeping may endure for the night, but JOY does come in the morning. I trust His way. I cannot understand it, or explain it.

He holds my hand

Well, September 6, 2008 marked the one month anniversary to one of the most difficult months in Philip's life. I was thinking it over ... if I could just turn back the clock and change my mind about Philip having the nasopharyngeal flap repair!

I know what you are thinking! Romans 8:28 "And we know that all things work together for good..." Siiigh! Remind me of that at 2 a.m. while I watch Philip struggle to take a breath. Philip had a sleep study, and the specialist who read us the report said that he stops breathing about once every minute. Talk about being scared to sleep!! Philip did respond well to a CPAP, a mask that fits over his nose and mouth to force air and help him breathe. Now, how do you get an 8 year old to wear it? We're trying to "con" him into thinking he's a fireman, an astronaut, whatever it takes to make him think wearing his mask is a cool thing.

Well, like any "normal" mother, I just sat and cried over the whole thing. What I wouldn't do just to turn back the clock.

I was reminded, then, that even here God is holding my hand. I cannot see Him, I cannot hear Him, but I know He is with me. Someone asked Philip if he remembered having tubes on him/in him and the scary moments after his surgery. He said, "No, I just remember God was holding my hand."

I need you more

I need you more, more than yesterday…

That is another beautiful chorus that goes like this:

I need you more, more than yesterday
I need you more, more than words can say
I need you more, than ever before
I need you more, Lord, I need you more

Those words could sum up my heart the few weeks after his flap surgery.

First off, life has been rough. In spite of using the CPAP at night, Philip continues to have periodic struggles with his breathing. He is rolling around at night, sitting up in his sleep trying to breathe with the stinky mask on his face.

I've had words with God. I just did not know what to do. I try to adjust his mask, reposition him, hold him, but nothing helps. Finally, I guess in desperation I broke down before God. "Would you just give me a sign, just show me that you know we are here? Just do something, anything?"

Silence

There was nothing. Sure weekends are filled with messages, prayers, friends, radio ministries, devotions that all minister to me, but nothing helps at 3 a.m. when you are desperate for an answer.

I can't quite explain it, but I know there is a greater good to come out of all this suffering. Two things I was reminded of: worship and healing can take place any time. I expect those to occur during a time of worship on Sunday morning. However, if I've not lived with the expectation on Monday to Saturday, how can I expect God to work just when I worship on Sunday? Worship is a lifestyle. May God give me a steadfast spirit, a right spirit to worship daily in every choice, every decision, in life every day.

Second, I watched a cartoon version of Abraham and the sacrifice of Isaac with my children. It all kind of clicked when I thought of Abraham's act of worship in sacrificing his son of promise, Isaac.

Wow. What faith in that man! I wonder if Sarah knew that the Lord commanded Abraham to sacrifice their son? The promised heir? Yet, Abraham knew God had a plan for Isaac. He knew the Lord would provide the lamb to be sacrificed, and that he and Isaac together would return from the mountain afterwards. God is in control. I pray that my faith, my trust may increase in these days, knowing the promise that is to be fulfilled in Philip's life.

Worship While I'm Waiting

I was talking to Philip one evening in 2008, about responsibility! Whew! It's definitely a foreign concept to an 8 year old. However, he does exhibit responsibility in taking care of his family and friends. He has a difficult time in taking care of his own self, occasionally. For instance, he frequently misplaces his glasses, his prosthetic ear, and at times his prosthetic eye. It drives me crazy. He will inevitably lose something on a day we are running late for school or church or some other important event. I continue to try to drill it into him that he must take care of his own things, because no one else will do this for him. Siiiigh!!!

Well, I said all that to give you some background on our talk the other evening. I told Philip, "You know one day, Phil, your ear is not going to come off your head. And one day you will see everything with both eyes. Do you believe that?" He answered, "Yeah, but when?" I told him, "I don't know when, Phil, but I know that God has heard our prayer, and the things that are impossible with humans are possible with God." Philip stunned me with his astute response," I know there is nothing too hard for the Lord." (That was another verse he learned years ago).

I guess this was just another word of encouragement and faith to me from my son. I have lately been hearing the song "While I'm Waiting." I don't think I really paid attention to the lyrics before when I've heard the song.

Basically, though the "wait" is painful, the "wait" is not easy, I will move ahead in obedience and worship and serve while I am waiting. I encourage you, friends, whatever you are waiting and seeking God for, as it is according to His will, keep serving; keep worshiping while you are waiting. He is an on-time God; He is not early, not late, but always an on-time God.

Praise it Up!!

There is more to tell you about how the Lord is my strength and my deliverer. One Friday night, one of our young people from church, Ruby, organized a benefit concert for Siskin Children's Institute, the school Philip attended for 5 years. The event, called "Praise it Up!" was a part of her senior project, and as her interest is in helping educate autistic children, she chose Siskin as the beneficiary of her concert.

She asked Philip to share some of his thoughts and experiences from Siskin during the concert. Philip initially told me, "Mom, I'll be so embarrassed!" I told him that I would stand on the stage with him. He took some comfort in that.

Ruby also asked me to share the vision of Love Without Reason® (LWR) as it was birthed in part from our own experiences with Philip. Needless to say, Philip and I were both preparing for the big event, and were excited. However, I was a little more anxious than I anticipated, I guess. All I could think about was how much I missed my husband who was in India during the time.

Whenever we are asked to speak about LWR or share Philip's testimony, we always spend some time in prayer before the event. I missed that and felt that I needed help that day. Well, before Philip and I entered the auditorium, I told him that we should just pray together. I reminded Philip of a scripture that he memorized from Jeremiah 1:4-10. In it, God tells Jeremiah not to be afraid, because God is with him. He also told the prophet that "I have put my words in your mouth." So as Philip was praying he said, "God please put your words in OUR mouths, mommy's and mine." His prayer so blessed and encouraged me. Then in the auditorium friends and family came also and encouraged me, stating they were praying for us.

The concert was like a church service, it was beautiful, and so easy to just praise God in that place. I thank God for his gentle reminders, and the way He speaks to us, sometimes even from the mouths of babes.

April 30, 2009

Guest entry by Santhosh Mathews

Since I cannot contain my joy... and I have to share it with the world... I am writing this to all of you from Erlanger hospital. I am right by Philip's bed side and just soaking in God's love.

Tonight, April 30, 2009, is one of the happiest nights of my life. Tonight in his hospital bed Philip accepted the Lord Jesus as his personal savior.

It happened in a wonderful way. After all the visitors had left his room, Philip turned to me and asked "Pappa, if I die will I be in heaven forever and ever?" I was speechless for a moment and then the Lord gave me words to tell him about what Jesus said about eternity. I shared with him the passage from Romans 10:9-13 and told him that when we with our mouths confess that Jesus Christ is Lord, and with our hearts believe that God raised Jesus from the dead, we will be saved.

Philip looked at me with his big round eye and asked what "saved" meant.

I shared with him from John 3:15,16 that God loved us so much that He sent His Son Jesus Christ into this world so that whoever believes in Jesus will not perish but have eternal life. Jesus in his prayer in John 17:3 reveals that eternal life is knowing God the Father and his son Jesus Christ.

In John 14:1-3, Jesus promises us that he is going to His Father's house to prepare a place for those who believe in Him and God. Jesus then goes on to say that He is coming back to take us with Him that we may be where He is. The Bible says that when we trust in Jesus Christ after hearing the message of salvation, we are sealed with the Holy Spirit of God who guarantees our inheritance until the redemption of our soul (Ephesians 1:13-14).

Then without my prompting my Philip simply closed his eye and prayed ... *"Jesus, I invite you to come into my heart so that I can live with you forever and ever. Amen."* And that was it!!! What a beautiful and a simple way this innocent life was led to the Lord. You do not need to know the entire Bible to accept the Lord into your heart. Just a simple invitation is enough.

I am so happy tonight that he allowed this to happen. God is good that he allowed me to lead my son to the way of Salvation. What the devil meant for evil... the Lord turned it around for good. For the past 9 months Philip was having trouble breathing and so we had to go back into surgery to help open up his airway so that he can breathe properly. Last time he almost lost his life on the surgery table, but this time he entered eternal life by accepting Jesus into his heart as his personal Lord and Savior. Salvation is truly a beautiful experience.

Philip and his ancestors

I thought you all might laugh at this event that happened sometime back. Philip and I work very diligently on homework once I return home from work. Every week he receives 5-7 new vocabulary words that he must know and understand and be able to use in a sentence. The teachers correlate the lessons with the vocabulary, I guess, to help the kids understand and prepare for their tests.

So they were studying in science the early Earth and fossils and dinosaur era. Apparently there was discussion about the "early ancestors" of the elephants, who were the wooly mammoths. The vocabulary word was ancestor. I thought that he understood the definition. This was verified during the family prayer that evening when Philip prayed for each grandparent and "bless all my ancestors." No one could keep a straight face during the prayer. Of course, Philip's innocent response with innocent eyes is, "What?"

It was so funny to hear, but in one way, I had to be glad because he did do well on that vocabulary test! :)

Revelation... out of the mouths of babes

Well, you've read some of the silly and humorous comments from Philip. To be just, I should let you know of the serious, thoughtful ones as well. :) My son is so sweet.

One Sunday in church after our Pastor had spoken about resolutions and taught about the correct paths to take in our daily walk with God, Philip rushed up to Santhosh in tears. He cried and apologized for "being a bad boy." My husband wasn't sure what Philip was referring to, but told him to wait and we will talk about it when we get home. As we were on the way home, Philip said "I'm sorry for being a bad boy since 2001." I laughed at his comment and said, "Ok, Philip but who said you were not a bad boy in 2000?" I did not understand what he was trying to say.

As we were eating lunch, Philip explained he had read the 10 commandments during the church service. He cried and said "I did not obey the 5th commandment to honor my parents. I'm sorry for being a bad boy." It was yet another teaching moment about God's grace and forgiveness. The Bible says we all have sinned and fallen short of God's glory (Romans 3:23), yet Christ came to rescue the lost and give beauty for ashes. Unfortunately, even we the churched people do not recognize such a revelation of our own unworthiness of such an Awesome God.

Jeremiah 32:27

Philip's promise verse for the New Year was Jeremiah 32:27

"Behold, I am the LORD, the God of all flesh: is there anything too hard for me?"

We asked him, well, what is the answer to this question? His response: "Absolutely nothing!"

Philip was an amazing encouragement and blessing of faith as we prepared for his surgery early 2010. Before the surgery we reminded him of this promise verse. While in the surgery waiting room, he spoke to other toddlers and their parents. We could hear him encouraging other parents. "This is my 16th surgery. My brother and sister are worried about me, but I know I'll be fine." Philip also said out loud in the waiting room to Santhosh and me, "Why don't you guys tell everybody how God helped me in my surgeries and healed me?" So we took a few minutes to share with a family sitting next to us about how God worked marvelously in Philip's life in the past, and how we know God will continue to work in the future.

Philip had no trouble coming out of anesthesia. He takes a little longer to recover from it, but he did well. Plus, we did NOT have to go to ICU this trip! Plus, we *were* discharged home due to his recovery. Our God is a prayer answering God.

I still have a lot to learn from my little son. It is so true how God said in his word; we must have the faith of a child.

Philip's Question

After recovering from surgery, Philip returned to school. He still had some swelling around his eye lid and the stitches had not dissolved yet. There were a few stitches around the ear implant as well. However, he tolerated this first week back to school. He was extremely concerned that he will have to learn all the letters "in cursive" and he was now behind. :) How lovely to be in third grade again!

Philip became more and more introspective. His questions were straightforward yet deep. One day, Philip, Santhosh and I were talking after we had cleaned Philip's eye and put on the antibiotic ointment. It is not usually a painful cleaning, but this time it hurt a little. He asked us, "If there is nothing too hard for the Lord, then why do I have to have surgery?"

Well, I was pretty stunned, and could not respond. Santhosh told him that the Bible tells us the things that are impossible with men, are possible with God. This is our hope and our peace, he said. When the doctors told us that "there is no hope your baby will be born alive," we knew that there is nothing too hard for our God. Now when our spine doctor says there is no way Philip's back can be straightened even with surgery, we know that the things that are impossible with men are possible with our God.

Philip's First (known) Convert

One Wednesday as we were driving back from church, I overheard a conversation between Philip and his then six-year-old sister, Sara. He questioned her about her own salvation. The conversation went something like this:

P: Sara, did you ask Jesus into your heart?

S: Yeah, yeah...I know what that means.

P: Sara, you have to repeat what I say.

S: Ok, you have to repeat what I say.

P: Sara! I'm serious. Pray like this, Jesus...

S: Jesus...

P: Please come into my heart.

S: Please come into my heart.

P: I want you to live in my heart forever.

S: I want you to live in my heart forever.

P: And never ever leave my heart.

S: And never ever leave my heart.

P: In Jesus' name..amen

S: In Jesus' name..amen.

Well, I couldn't believe what I heard. This is the first time I've heard him share salvation with anyone. I had shared Philip's efforts in evangelization with one of his uncles and his response was, "Well, Philip needs to get his own household saved, then he will move on throughout the world." I pray so. Philip has tried to speak to one of his classmates about Jesus but that child, according to Philip, wanted to believe in his own "false god."

I have heard of young children getting up on the pulpits in other countries and sharing the Gospel with the people. God is moving in the hearts of these young ones. Pray for them. Out of their mouths the Lord has perfected praise and ordained strength. May God help each of us to do our part in these last days to fulfill God's ultimate plan.

Another one of Philip's questions

"What is it like to have two eyes," he asked during a haircutting session. Well, what is my world like since I have two eyes? Did I even know of a difference?

My little son did. His innocent question broke my heart. How many things I take for granted that he just wonders "what it's like?" I had to ask myself, how many things do I miss because I have two eyes? How many things do I look over because I have two eyes? I wish I could say that I see everything because of my two eyes, but I do not. A lot of times, we don't have to have the eyes to see that someone hurts or is confused or sad. We make the choice whether we want to see or not.

I've seen Philip talk to strangers and ask them what is wrong, just because he notices they appear stressed or hurt. This happens while I, who have two eyes, would look past them and not stop to ask them anything. I guess life with two eyes is not much different than having one eye. It all matters on if you choose to see.

Need to Know Basis

God knows what the future holds, and I do not 'need to know.' I was reminded of God's faithfulness by an evangelist one morning on his radio program.

His Word is a lamp to our feet, and a light to our paths. We do not know what our final destination and goal is, but we do have enough light for the next step.

Philip met with his spine surgeon for his six month follow up. We wanted to see how his curve measured out now. Unfortunately, his curve had advanced to 102 degrees. Our doctor was concerned about heart and lung function.

I could not stop weeping that afternoon. On our way back home, we stopped at the church to just seek God. Later that evening, as I prayed with Philip, I heard his prayer. "God, I know you turned the water into wine. I still believe you can make my back straight."

Need to know. I wish I knew the final destination for Philip and his spine, but I was reminded, it's a need to know basis. I have enough light for the step that I am on, and I will trust Him to help us move to the next step.

Take no Thought

One part of a recent Sunday message was 'take no thought.' This is in reference to Matthew 6 where Jesus tells us to take no thought for tomorrow, or for our lives, or for the substances of life. INSTEAD, seek FIRST the kingdom of God, and his righteousness and all these things will be added to you.

You may know the story of King Nebuchadnezzar's dream from Daniel 2. He has this dream and can't remember it, then threatens to kill his magicians unless they reveal it to him. Amazing. Anyway, through God, Daniel reveals the dream and the interpretation, which basically talks about the Kingdom of God and the counterfeit kingdom that the enemy tries to set up in our lives. We read that a stone which was carved out of the mountain without hands, was the destroyer of this counterfeit kingdom.

I guess one part that resonated for me was the message to not worry about tomorrow. I felt strengthened to believe that God was healing Philip. I believed it and praised God believing He has already healed him "without hands." I couldn't get that image out of my head.

Then Monday evening I heard the answering machine, and Philip's spine doctor had called wanting to know if we had reconsidered the new kind of spine surgery discussed at a previous office visit. I couldn't believe the timing of this phone call. They could not call me any other time, but right after I felt so confirmed that God was healing Philip. But even after the phone call, I just felt even more so that God had begun an amazing work.

O Happy Day

We had the opportunity last weekend to take our family visiting us from India out to Gatlinburg, a tourist attraction that is close to home. To view the attractions on the streets of Gatlinburg and Pigeon Forge, you basically park your car, and walk to your destinations.

So towards the end of the outing as we were preparing to return home, we began the long walk back to the parking garage. As we were all walking on the streets, Philip was singing joyfully "O happy day, happy day, when Jesus washed my sins away..!!!" And he kept repeating that one line over and over. He was singing so loudly and innocently. I saw many people do a double take as they passed him by and heard his song.

I could not help but smile. That's real evangelization, I believe. Say it as it is, no questions. And say it joyfully, even though you are not 'normal looking' but your message and behavior says you are happy in spite of it all.

I wish I had his courage. I would be happy to leave tracts in the bathrooms and rest areas. That would be the extent of my evangelization. I pray that my passion would shift to rescue, restore and offer the salvation of Jesus to as many lives as I could while I have the time on this earth.

And as Jesus passed by, he saw a man which was blind from his birth.

And his disciples asked him, saying, "Master, who did sin, this man, or his parents, that he was born blind?"

Jesus answered, "Neither hath this man sinned, nor his parents: but that the works of God should be made manifest in him."

- ***John 9:1-3***

A God moment?

In the preparations for the Trinidad mission trip, members of our church met for prayer and intercession. As our friends Sam, Sheaba, Philip and myself were gathered for prayer, we somehow got on the topic of 'choose life' and the recent bible study we had with Pastor Michael Mathew. The study topic was "Dealing with Sin." We talked about death and life.

In speaking about life, our reference was from Romans 6. I did not have my notes with me, and just shared 'obedience' as the starting place for choosing life, because that was the only point I could remember at the time of the prayer. Then I mentioned what I thought could follow obedience and that was righteousness and holiness. Suddenly, while the three of us were trying to think of the correct order of the points, Philip pipes up and says so "obedience unto righteousness and righteousness unto holiness and holiness unto life, right?" You should have seen our faces with mouths wide open.

To this day, I do not know how Philip knew the correct order and the keyword "unto" which I did not even mention during the prayer! He was not at the Bible study when Pastor Michael was here. I believe it was definitely a "God moment" and we were being reminded through the mouth of this child.

This is actually what Philip has studied and prayed for. He memorized several of the first few verses of Jeremiah chapter

1, where the Lord calls Jeremiah into ministry and tells him "I will put my words in your mouth." I believe the Lord has started His work.

Later I asked Philip how he knew those four points of "Life." And his response was "God told me."

I believe him.

He knows my Name

Philip has been singing the song, "He knows my name." If you don't know the words:

I have a Father
He formed my heart
Before even time began
My life was in His hands

He knows my name
He knows my every thought
He sees each tear that falls
And hears me when I call

Hearing Philip sing the song reminded me of events surrounding his own heart before he was even born. I was thinking about my classmates in nursing school advising me of new in-vitro surgery that could be performed on a baby's heart, even before the baby is born.

I remembered talking to the cardiologist who told us there were so many holes in Philip's heart, he couldn't even count them. I remembered crying because of the heart medicine I was giving him after he was born. I thought of one of those routine visits with the cardiologist where the chest x-ray demonstrated his heart size returning to normal. And the doctor telling us, *"whatever you all are doing, keep on doing it, because it's working!"*

I remembered laying my hand over Philip's heart and just praying for healing of all the holes in his heart.

In the follow-up ultrasound of Philip's heart, no holes were identified! Without any surgery all the holes had closed on their own! Our Father, the One who formed Philip's heart, had healed him.

And the same is true for each of us. God knows our name, our thoughts, sees our tears, and hears our cries. May God help us and encourage us through His word and songs.

East Hamilton, here we come!

Those are the words Philip shouted one Friday at 6:15 in the morning! We had received an invitation to share Philip's testimony at our local high school's Fellowship of Christian Athletes gathering. While I was extremely excited about the opportunity that my cousin, who was a junior at the high school, presented, I was concerned about Philip's reaction.

I wondered how he would feel with the sixth through twelfth grade students that would be present in their auditorium. Initially, he told me that he did not want to go to the high school. I asked him, "What's the difference in sharing your testimony in Chattanooga versus Trinidad?" And with that he said, "I'll do it!"

I shared in brief Philip's testimony and showed the kids Philip's baby album. We only had 15 minutes that morning before the students began their day at school. Afterwards, I invited Philip to come to the front to greet everyone. He said Hello, and then he told them he wanted to sing a song for them. He sang "He knows my name." As we were practicing this song the day before, Philip improvised the chorus to say

> *He knows Your name*
> *He knows Your every thought*
> *He sees each tear that falls*
> *And hears You when You call*

He told me that he wanted to end the song with this chorus to encourage the kids. I told him he could do whatever he wanted with the song. It went perfectly.

As it turned out, we learned that morning that one of their students had been accidentally shot and killed the previous night. The school was in mourning. I believe that God wanted us there for such a time as this. I explained to the students, that my anchor in the time of my personal tragedy and sorrow was the Word of God. This Word does not change. People change. Life happens. Things move on. But the Word of God will never change. That is a Rock that I held on when my life was turned upside down. I encouraged them to also hold on the Word in the middle of their sorrow and tragedy.

Pray for our children. They go through so much these days in school. May God help them to hold on, and may His grace strengthen them each day.

An interview

As we were interviewed by a gentleman in Trinidad who broadcasts on a local radio station, he asked Philip, "What do you want people to know about your life?" Philip's response was very simple. "People need to know that God answers prayer. Sometimes He may say yes, sometimes He may say no. But God answers prayers. My parents have been praying for my spine. And every time they pray, I know that my back is getting healed by one degree."

Santhosh and I were stunned. We did not prep Philip, nor did we even know the questions beforehand that were to be asked. It was God who 'put the words in his mouth.'

We praise God for His infallible Word. It is full of power!! We will believe and hold to what the Lord says, and not what our physical eyes see.

Westview's got LOTS of Talent!

The third annual school fundraiser, Westview's Got Talent, is a talent demonstration of teachers, and students selected through audition. There were ventriloquist acts, acrobatics, musical and singing talents displayed. This happened to be our first talent show we were able to attend. As you may have guessed, our eyes were shining for our children, especially to see a fulfillment of words spoken over Philip's life years ago.

Philip is living up to his name, as an evangelist. When he auditioned for the show several weeks prior, his music teacher had tears in her eyes, as she heard Philip state in his words his brief testimony. He then sang his famous chorus "He knows my name." No one had known of the story behind Philip's life till then.

What started out as a simple request from a Westview parent, turned into a message of hope and encouragement for the audience. A video of Philip's program is on the www.lovewithoutreason.org website.

The ministry has begun for Philip. The message is "Go, preach the good news...."

Have you checked your mailbox lately?

School field trips are making me broke!! Philip had his end of the year field trip scheduled, which cost $20. Multiply this times 3 children and at least 5 field trips. It adds up quickly!

Anyway, I told him to ask Santhosh for the money. Santhosh asked him to ask God for the money. "You never know, Philip, God could just send you a check in the mailbox."

Thursday morning before we drove off to school, Santhosh asked Philip if he had checked the mailbox. Philip ran back excitedly saying "God answered my prayer! He gave me $20!!" There was no question in Philip's mind. He never even asked if we put the money in the mailbox.

With all the struggles and breathing issues and the new recommendation by one of our doctors that Philip needs a breathing tube inserted into his neck surgically, I wept when I was reminded of the verse from Matthew 7:11.

"If you, then, though you are evil, know how to give good gifts to your children, how much more will your Father in heaven give good gifts to those who ask him!"

Oh, to have the faith of a child! Though the weeks have been hard to see and bear, if I being evil know to give good gifts to my son, how much more does my Abba Father give good gifts to those who ask?

I'm so thankful for the encouragement and blessing of God's word. He is my faithful Father. I pray that you believe Him, at His Word. He is real, dear readers. He loves you. He knows your name. Believe him.

Now, go check your mailbox!!

What was Hagar thinking?

Philip has been dealing with a horrible upper respiratory infection for two weeks. To add to it, he has had this horrible cough, and now nasal congestion. Over a period of 3 nights, I watched him sleep. He would toss and turn, intermittently wake up and talk in his sleep. It was a very depressing few nights to the point that I was dreading nighttime. All I could do after tucking Philip in for the night was kneel at his bed and cry to God. It broke my heart to see him struggle so much to breathe. I tried cleaning his nose, using the nasal emollients we have used in the past, but nothing was helping.

Finally, after praying I returned to my bed. I couldn't sleep, but my mind just went to Hagar and her son, Ishmael from Genesis 21. Hagar finds shade for her son Ishmael in the wilderness after being kicked out of her home, then she goes "a good way off" supposedly so she wouldn't see him suffer. I wondered how she must have felt. Nowhere to turn, nobody to give an answer or provide water for her son. It was a desperate situation.

I prayed reminding myself that "God, you gave us this gift. Now, I've done all I know to do, Philip belongs to You, YOU must help him." Then I walked back to my room. He struggled all night with his sleep.

I even went looking for that old breathing machine, the CPAP. I could not find the mask to go over his face. Philip was not happy about me mentioning the CPAP and did not want to wear it.

I reminded him of his promise verse for the year. Jeremiah 32:27 says "*I am the God of all flesh, is there anything too hard for me?*" We prayed together, believing in a peaceful night of sleep, because there is nothing too hard for our God. He still struggled, but I felt he rested better than the nights before.

Hagar's cry

The other night Philip fell asleep on our bed. He began to toss and turn and breathe restlessly and gasp. As you know by now, this is not new, however, he cannot use oxygen by the nasal cannula, and so we have helplessly been watching him sleep this way. Some nights he may seem to rest more peacefully. This night was one of the bad nights. I woke up several times during the night trying to readjust him and prop him up on pillows. Nothing would help him. After being kicked again, and trying to reposition him, I finally got up and moved to another room, and left him with Santhosh.

I cried all the way to the other room. Why, Oh, God, Why? It just made me think of Hagar, in the book of Genesis. She and her son were cast out of Abraham's house with a jug of water, which soon ran out in the desert. She leaves her son in one place, and then goes off in another direction saying, "I don't want to watch my son die." Genesis 21 reads that God heard the voice of the son, though nothing is mentioned about what he might have said. I wondered how Hagar felt turning her back away from her son, in his suffering. I felt awful about turning from Philip, but I didn't know what else to do. Praying, rebuking the enemy, crying. Nothing seemed to change his situation. I began to ask God just to breathe his breath of life into Philip.

Next afternoon I was talking to Philip and he said "I thank God for giving me a good night of rest, Mom. The Bible says He gives sleep to his saints, and so He is giving me good sleep." I guess in spite of what I actually see in Philip's sleep pattern, he does get good rest.

Though there are so many things I cannot understand with regard to Philip and his health, I know God the Father loves him more than I do. He has Philip in His hand. His purpose will be accomplished, and nothing will change that.

Hagar's eyes

I guess that I shouldn't leave myself thinking about Hagar's tears. One night at church I heard a great thought about Hagar's eyes, and it encouraged me. If you read her story in Genesis 21, you see that she was weeping because there was nothing to feed her son with in the wilderness. She left her son under some shrubs, and walked away crying. The angel of God speaks to her and says "God has heard the boy's voice." And the next verse says God opened her eyes, and she saw a well of water.

The well had been there before, it was just that her eyes were not opened to see it. Even for us, we pray for a miracle in our life and in our situations. Sometimes, however, the miracle is right in front of us, it's just that our eyes aren't opened.

Philip had his sleep study, and the recommendation was for him to wear a BIPAP to sleep. We are working with him in getting used to the apparatus. I praise God that there was no recommendation for a tracheotomy; I will claim it as a miracle that was right in front of me. Now, I am waiting to see a miracle in regards to his spine. The miracle is right in front of my eyes, I believe it!!

One Generation Praising Him to the Next Generation

We live in a time of great appreciation for the younger, faster, attractive and youthful bodies. But we would be remiss to think that our elders should be ignored. With our Philip we needed 24/7 supervision, especially after his surgeries. With both of us working, we thank God for both sets of our parents, the Mathews' and the Ponnachens', who sacrificed their time, jobs, and their own personal needs to help us and to be a rock of support for us.

Their spiritual walk and life stories especially are a mold for us to follow. As is written in Psalm 145:4, *"One generation shall praise thy works to another, and shall declare thy mighty acts."*

In the examples of their lives, and the way God has led them in the past, we are strengthened to know how God will also lead us. And so the circle continues to the next generation! It gives each of us even more reason to be mindful of the legacy we leave our children.

Look at the RAINBOW!!!

I was driving Philip home from school one dreary rainy day. Philip was happily chattering about his day, and then he mentioned his most embarrassing moment in Bible class. He had fallen asleep in class!!! His instructor had kindly advised him to go to the first aid station, but Philip told me that he resolved that would never happen again!

For several days Philip has really struggled with his breathing at night, while wearing his BIPAP. Like I've said before, it is so difficult to watch him struggle. I feel so helpless in watching, repositioning, or holding him. There is nothing to do but cry and pray that he would rest well so that he would be refreshed the next morning.

I couldn't help but get teary-eyed when Philip told me about his embarrassing moment in class. I again thought to myself, which doctor should I talk to, and how else could we correct things or help him? Suddenly, Philip shouted, "Mom, look, look ahead!" I panicked, thinking I was heading for a car. Then he shouted, "Look at the rainbow, it's a reminder of God's promises!"

It was indeed a beautiful rainbow, and we saw two together, in fact. I thought of the promises obtained over the years. Many promises over the future of Philip and the miracles in the past, and the miracles we believe to come.

There is no such thing as coincidence. This was a providential reminder, God does keep his promises. People fail us, things, life, nothing is for certain. But God. His Word never fails.

Stay strong, my friends. God is on the throne, and He never changes.

Sunsets

Just like no two fingerprints or no two snowflakes are alike, no two sunsets are alike. As I was leaving my job one night, walking through the parking lot, I could not help but notice the beautiful sunset. It was a gorgeous set of colors. I love looking at sunsets. I always have. It's been very unusual that over the past few years, I've noticed that on several occasions when I am feeling at an all time low, and searching for answers that I will notice a beautiful sunset.

It's almost like the rainbow in the sky and the promise of no more flooding as Noah received in the story found in the book of Genesis.

I was reading a book, and the author was saying how much she loved starfish. I can't remember the book title, but she was going through personal struggles and as she was on the beach crying, she came to a cove that was filled with.....you guessed it, starfish!

She was encouraging the readers that God knows and understands our hearts. He ministers and speaks to us in different ways. I know that through the sunsets, God has been gently reminding me that He is in control.

I was encouraged by a friend's testimony regarding her job. In my issues with my job, I know I serve a God who creates something out of nothing. He reminded me with that sunset. I know my God is in control. He is a Creator who transforms emptiness and nothingness to fullness and beauty. Though this is a hard journey and difficult lesson to understand, I know He hears me when I call. The reminder was in the sunset.

Walking for LIFE!

One Saturday Philip joined in the annual Walk for Life to benefit Choices Pregnancy Resource Center. I talked to him beforehand about how some babies are "born" before their time and die because the mom and dad are scared or worried or different other reasons. I reminded him that every life is valuable and the Bible teaches that children are a gift from God. So if he believes that, he can participate in the walk. He agreed, even when I told him the walk was two miles.

He did get fatigued about every half mile. He stopped for a rest break and a back massage. The young women who came from church to walk all encouraged him to keep on walking. Philip encouraged himself saying "I'm not giving up, I'm going to walk!" And he continued until he completed the two mile walk!

His simple understanding of the importance of life and how we all are children of God was invigorating. To have that kind of passion and pursuit for the sake of the children is something we adults MUST copy in our lives.

"The Spirit of the Lord G<small>OD</small> is upon me; because the L<small>ORD</small> hath anointed me to preach good tidings unto the meek; he hath sent me to bind up the brokenhearted, to proclaim liberty to the captives, and the opening of the prison to them that are bound;

To proclaim the acceptable year of the L<small>ORD</small>, and the day of vengeance of our God; to comfort all that mourn;

To appoint unto them that mourn in Zion, to give unto them beauty for ashes, the oil of joy for mourning, the garment of praise for the spirit of heaviness; that they might be called trees of righteousness, the planting of the L<small>ORD</small>, that he might be glorified.

And they shall build the old wastes, they shall raise up the former desolations, and they shall repair the waste cities, the desolations of many generations."

\- ***Isaiah 61:1-4 [KJV]***

Mumbai is mine

If you have noticed the mission of Love Without Reason®, you know that our heart is directed toward helping and restoring the lives of victims of sex trafficking and children with craniofacial birth defects. We (as a family) had the opportunity to go back to India and visit with great-grandparents, and also meet with and network with people with a passion similar to LWR.

On the plane ride as we landed in Mumbai (Bombay) en route to our grandparent's home in Kerala, I heard the pilot announce that we would be landing shortly in Mumbai airport. It was very early morning and I was amazed at the way Mumbai was all "lit" up. That was just a beautiful view looking down from the dark sky. I don't know why, but the thought hit me at that time of what kind of evil goes on in this particular city, specifically I mean sex trafficking of the children.

I just began to cry and pray in the Spirit for the children who at that very moment may be tormented, disheartened, and depressed. "God let someone give them hope right now and don't let anyone feel there is no hope." I remember praying that. I decided then that Mumbai is mine.

I heard a message that weekend where the pastor encouraged and commanded us to "stand in the evil day" (Ephesians 6:13). THIS IS THE EVIL DAY! When children are betrayed or deceived and lose their innocence to become slaves to people who cheat, threaten, drug, and use their bodies and discard them like trash. Oh, may God help us in this evil day!! Though I've used the phrase "Mumbai is mine" for some time, part of me asks the question "What am I thinking? Do I know what I'm up against?"

An example of standing in the evil day, from John 18:2-4 illustrates Jesus in the garden of Gethsemane with the soldiers approaching with their lanterns, torches and weapons. Jesus does not wait for them to introduce themselves! He goes forth and asks them "who are you looking for?" That is standing in the evil day. No matter what evil is against us, if I have submitted my will to God, I will stand in the evil day.

And Mumbai is mine! Join me in interceding daily for the children of Mumbai.

Intercession!!

I heard on the radio recently of yet another instance of young people enslaved in sex trafficking. It was a typical scenario.

A pastor and family serving God in Pakistan as missionaries apparently were having financial struggles. Their oldest two children, 14 and 17 year old sisters, desired to help the family by searching for employment through simple jobs. A "trusted" neighbor told the father (the pastor) of a particular easy job in the town that would fit the children. He did not want them to go, however, the children persuaded him, and he finally gave in. Of course, you know the story. The neighbor sold them to a brothel, where they immediately were repeatedly violated and sexually assaulted. The good news is that the young women were rescued.

The bad news is that now those dear young women must psychologically, emotionally and physically heal. I grieve for that father, as well. Would you commit to praying for them daily? May God give them peace and healing, that only He can do. There is nothing and no one in the world who can grant peace like Jesus can. Amen?

What is that old gospel song, "Can't nobody do me like Jesus?" God is faithful. Even in the hardest, most grievous, most questioning of times, He still promises to never leave us or forsake us. Please pray that the parents and those young girls will know that, and know that God has them engraved in His hands. They have been rescued for a purpose, and may God help them to be in His perfect will.

O Holy Night

My favorite Christmas song of all time is O Holy Night. One of the verses talks about the mission that Christ had in coming to earth.

"Chains shall He break, for the slave is our brother;

and in His name, all oppression shall cease."

I shared this during a Christmas program, how **we** may as the churched or unchurched population be enslaved to things. Whether its food, pornography, alcohol, or our selfishness, we can be under bondage to these things. Christ has come not that we be oppressed, but be free. If Christ sets us free, we are free indeed, according to the Word. You can read from the prophecy in Isaiah 61, Christ has come to bind up the brokenhearted (can I get a witness in here?), release the captive, comfort the ones who mourn.

I could not help but think of my LWR babies who also are under bondage through sexual slavery. Every one of them needs to know that Christ loves them and died for them, and has come to set the captive free. So many times they are psychologically tormented to believe that no one can release them and no one will accept them if they run away from the stronghold of the pimp. Please commit to praying for these dear children and young people. They can be set free, physically and spiritually. Pray for the part that LWR will play also in these things. God has promised He will teach and instruct us in LWR's part to rescue and restore lives out of oppression into freedom.

The story that haunted me today

I had a few extra minutes one morning in November to iron my clothes and prepare for work after we sent the kids off to school. I happened to notice that my calendar above the ironing table was still on October. So I pulled down the calendar and a paper about National Orphan Sunday fell out. I stopped to read a story about a couple who decided to become foster parents. They wanted to house and care for kids who were abandoned or had no parents to care for them, until the state government finds someone to adopt them.

So one day this couple gets the call to see if they can on an emergency basis take care of a young boy named Duane (not real name). They agree to and Duane comes to their home. He spends several days there and begins to get comfortable. The mother of the house goes one morning to do the laundry in the laundry room, and he follows her. When he sees her pick up the bleach bottle, he immediately screams, "Please don't put it in my eyes, please, I've been a good boy." She immediately drops everything to console and comfort him.

I wept after reading the story. And all day long while at work and at home, I could not get the story out of my head. I began to pray for the hundreds of thousands and perhaps millions of children who are orphaned, physically tortured, sexually abused, neglected and hungry.

What kind of life these children are leading in their homes. What kind of future or hope is there for them, if we do not get involved? We know our God is a God of restoration and hope. He offers hope, when all around us is hopelessness. Help us get the message out of God's unconditional love. Identify your area of expertise and be willing to step up and help change the destiny of one child **today**!

Trafficking Awareness Day

January 11 is Human Trafficking Awareness Day, and I had to tell you some of the amazing events in 2010/2011 that occurred in regards to trafficking.

First, when the mission team from Chattanooga Christian Assembly was in Guatemala, a few of us stretched our hands out over Antigua, a major sex trafficking city, and prayed specifically for rescue, restoration and spiritual awakening over the victims of this crime in Guatemala. I believe God has started a work already, and we were able to tag along in it.

Second, when the mission team was in Trinidad, they were amazingly given an opportunity to be in the forefront of prayer over Trinidad. A young woman with a burden for Trinidad's spiritual awakening had arranged for various ministries to meet in the heart of the capitol city every January morning from 5 am to 6 am and cry out and intercede on behalf of Trinidad. We were invited to start the prayer out on January 1. The heart of the city is the prime area of trafficking, and drug dealing.

But on January 1, 2011 that area was dealt a spiritual hit, with the prayers and tears, going up to God as a memorial. I believe God is moving mightily in Trinidad, already.

Third, I learned of a praise report in a local nonprofit organization, 1040 Connections, that fights sex trafficking in

Nepali borders. They reported in December that at the Nepal/India border they rescued a 16 year old girl from a trafficker. The trafficker was put in jail, and the girl was sent to a restoration home. Through the standard protocols of entering the restoration home, the young lady discovered she was pregnant. She is keeping the baby. Two other young women were rescued in the same border area. Both were found to be pregnant, and apparently one is leaning toward having an abortion. Their traffickers are still at large. Please pray for these young women and their babies. May God who is the God of all comfort, give them peace, comfort and grace to bear all things and make the best choices for their future.

Please intercede on behalf of the young boys, girls, men and women who are held in bondage in this 21st century. Christ has come to set the captives free. What is your part in this rescue, as you are the hands and feet of Christ? Pray that this is revealed to you.

PIMP

What a nasty word!

I couldn't believe my eyes when I was looking through Factory Card Outlet's Halloween costume catalog. You guessed it; there was a costume for 'pimp.' Who would want to be one? Even as a joke?

And yet, we hear the word used in various forms, to describe various things. Sometimes the word can also be used to glorify a person's appearance or to speak about someone in high terms.

To our young people who are tortured, abused, and enticed by these glorified hellions, the word pimp sends shudders of fear. I urge you to do everything to tear apart and put down this word. Educate people when they use the term to glorify a person. Tell them what pimps do. Tell them about the anguish and pain of young people. Tell them of the threats, the physical and sexual and emotional abuse that pimps place on our young people.

Tell them they are of the devil, because they know how to deceive and entice, and once the bait is taken, our young people are killed. All you have to do is look at the cages in Mumbai, or the hollow eyes of the street kids in Atlanta to understand the lack of value or respect of life by these pimps.

We learned that in red light districts of Mumbai, the boys who grow up as the sons of prostitutes end up becoming pimps for their moms. They are placed into the position of trying to solicit business for their mothers to make money. As this may be the only world these young men know, they know nothing different. There is no hope to be "an engineer, or a doctor when I grow up." There is nothing other than this kind of lifestyle in their futures.

The cycle can be broken! With the help of God, we will press on through Love Without Reason® until justice is served for the sake of the next generation.

Kamathipura – The Red Light District of Mumbai

In the bleak, dark brothel, there are silent cries, hopeless eyes, and tears that never run dry.

In the brothel, I had the opportunity to meet a middle aged woman who spoke my language and shared with me her story of how she ended up in the brothel. She was married and had four grown children who were obtaining their college education in Southern India. Her husband left her after losing a lot of money in a gambling scheme. She was left alone to manage her children and to keep them in their schools. A friend told her to travel to Mumbai to work in hotels and earn good money. They both went together, and after arriving in the brothel, she found out what exactly the new job would entail. She went on to explain how the first months were so difficult, and how she lived in fear for her life because of the abuse of the men who frequented the brothels. After two years of living in the brothel, she felt there was no alternative for her to earn similar income in any other job so that she could send money to her children and continue their education.

We pleaded with her to consider leaving the life of despair, and shared the hope we knew in Christ and the hope we had experienced with Philip's story. She heard us and allowed us to pray with her, but didn't leave. My heart weeps for her and other women like her who are prisoners of their circumstances.

The Spirit of the Lord is upon me, for he has anointed me to…set the captives free. These were the words I heard that morning. God has come to bind the broken hearted, and release the captives. He is a God of justice. Let God arise, and His enemies be scattered.

The boy I left behind

"Tap, tap, tap" was the noise I heard on my window in the backseat of the vehicle I was riding in through the streets of Bangalore in August of 2012. We had stopped at the traffic light. I turned to see a young man with two faint white stripes on his forehead and pleading eyes. His hands were full of toy Rubik cubes, and he tried to get me to purchase one.

I could not do anything for a few moments but look him in the eyes. I think he knew I felt pity for him. He didn't break my gaze for some time. The traffic light turned green, and I was advised by my family to tell him "no." I gently shook my head at him, as the car moved on.

The following Monday, we spent the day at Oasis India, Bangalore. We watched a documentary on child beggary. Apparently there is a beggary mafia who purchases children from the trafficking mafia in Bangalore. Oasis, several other non-governmental organization, the police department and government agencies banded together to rescue children who are forced to beg on the streets. Their results astonished me.

Children who were rescued in the raids ranged from ages infant to teenagers. Many had been kidnapped or sold into beggary, where they had "new parents." These parents forced the children to beg for money on busy streets and intersections.

One five year old boy said "My father makes me beg on the streets." He was asked what does father do with the money you give him? "He buys drinks," was the child's response.

One beautiful nine year old girl who was rescued did not want to return to her "parents." The "parents" did not bring appropriate documentation proving their parenthood to the courts. By chance, one of the government officials recognized the man who claimed to be her father as a man who had been in court previously claiming some other boys to be his sons.

This little girl not only was rescued, but she provided information that led to the discovery and rescue of her "brothers and sisters" who were living under plastic sheets on the street. The police were able to rescue several children because of her bravery.

How is it that people devalue life? They have torn these children from their families, and humiliated, hurt and beaten them. This documentary tore my heart. I immediately thought of the young man selling Rubik cubes. I wish I could have rescued him, rather than leaving him behind. Perhaps one day I will find him. Please pray for this young man and his safety.

Get involved in the rescue of the millions of child beggars around the world. This is a worthy cause.

An advocate for children

I happened to hear a testimony by the president of an organization dedicated to improvement of health outcomes and physical outcomes of children all around the world. This man's life was not the typical life with a "call" to ministry. He unfortunately suffered during his childhood with physical, emotional, and sexual abuse by the hands of people who ran a boarding school for missionary children in Africa. His parents were missionaries in Africa. He suffered for years; his childhood was robbed of innocence. He spoke of how as a third grader when he was being taught in his math class how to find the "average" of numbers; he averaged how many times he was physically beaten per week. The average was 17.

He shared with his audience the importance of a forgiving spirit. Many people can suffer at the hands of abusers and keep an unforgiving spirit which will result either in overachievers or those with a "beaten" attitude. Neither one is in the will of God. He said after returning to the US for good at age 17, "I was an enraged and bitter adolescent after suffering the years of abuse." One camp counselor at that time preached on how those we do not forgive will stay on our backs, rent-free, until we forgive them and let them go.

The message changed his life! He did not become an overachiever that is driven by the taunting voices of the abusers who told him he'll never make it. He did not become an underachiever either, believing the lies the abusers told him when they said he would not amount to anything. With God's help and grace to forgive the ones who abused him, he moved into the plan of God.

I had to pull my car over and weep over this powerful testimony. I think about the atrocities the innocent children suffer at the hands of people who either don't care or have no humanity in themselves. If LWR can just reach one child, my God, it will all be worth it. I urge you, readers, please do everything you can to bring hope and life to the lives of our children. Even the littlest things, do it for the sake of a child. Pray and intercede on behalf of others who are active as advocates for the children.

Generational Curses

I had the privilege to hear the life changing testimony of a former alcoholic, who also is my dear friend. He shared the fear he carried with him, knowing he descended from a family of alcoholics. Though his job exposed him to alcohol, he did not give in to the initial temptation. After his daughter's birth, he recalled praying over her life in tongues, rejoicing in what God had done for him. But slowly over time, he began to slip into the spiral of alcoholism.

His wife remembered how family dinners in restaurants had to be at alcohol serving restaurants. He added that throughout the daily work grind, he would be very anxious if the thought entered in his mind that he could possibly run out of alcohol. A life without alcohol terrified him. He felt as if he was in a pit filled with quicksand. The more he struggled to get out the more he felt being sucked into the pit.

His wife did not confront him, as she heard the Lord tell her not to say anything about the alcohol. She was advised to cover him in prayer, and to continue loving him. She remained obedient to the word she heard from God for over twenty years, even though it proved difficult to do so. He slowly started stepping away from church and the things of God. As his job location would change from city to city, he would try to start new, and stop drinking alcohol. He never was able to abstain, and always ended up back in the same spiral. Finally, he began to contemplate suicide.

Miraculously, he sought the Lord. As the Word says, "This poor man cried to the Lord, and He heard him, and saved him out of all his troubles" (Psalm 34:6). He remembered crying out to Jesus and telling him that if he ever set him free, he would serve him for the rest of his life. The Lord answered the cry of my friend in an instant. For the first time in over 20 years he did not crave alcohol. When he woke up the next day he had no seizures, or withdrawals, just complete freedom from the addiction of alcohol. He has never gone back since that day. He joyfully says, "That generational curse was broken through me! And it ends with me!"

Quoting from his favorite Psalm, he said "the Lord brought up my soul from the grave: He kept me alive, that I should not go down to that horrible pit. The Lord came to set me free. He came to bind up my broken heart. He has turned my mourning into dancing!" (Psalm 30)

No matter the addiction, sickness and disease we know the Lord Jesus Christ can set you free. Would you trust Him as my friend did?

Mothers Day 2010

I woke up this mother's day to rush to church for praise and worship preparation. The family was all awake by 8 a.m., but only Philip came and wished me a happy mother's day, before even brushing his teeth.

I've given mothers a lot of thought this past week. I had been a mother for ten years!! God is faithful and I'm grateful for the honor. I visited the National Memorial for the Unborn last week and couldn't help but cry as I read various memorials by moms and dads who were grieving over the children they had aborted. I had to stop and say a prayer for those moms. Then there is a memorial for the babies who were miscarried. So many women desire to be moms, yet have been unsuccessful. I had to remember those moms too. And then there are those women yet to be mothers. Pray for them as well, in faith believing they will one day be mothers.

You women give a lot of influence and hold so much in your hands in your daily ministering to your children. Never for a moment think you are just a "mom" or just a "woman." God has entrusted something so precious and unique to mothers. So much of a child's future and destiny is powerfully tied to the mother of that child. Speak positive words of influence to your children. At every available opportunity, guide them and instruct them on the ways of our God. Most importantly, be an example, a model of Christ's love for them on earth.

About Faith

I've been trying to understand faith. It is the substance of things hoped for and the evidence of things not seen (Hebrews 11:1). Faith is climbing up the staircase when you don't even see the stairwell. Prayer is the key to heaven, faith unlocks the door. There are so many things to say **about** faith.

One of my dearest friends, younger than me, has been childless for 6 years into her marriage. After a miscarriage, my heart broke for her and the grief I could only imagine in her heart. On a "Spirit of Faith" I bought maternity clothes for her believing that God would bless this loving couple with their first child. I held on to those maternity clothes for a little over a year, thinking I may be crazy or this "thought can't be from God." When I finally had the courage to give them to her, unbeknown to me, she was 4 months pregnant!

Now, seeing the fruit of her prayers, I question how can I apply this in my own life? Was what I did with those maternity clothes an act of faith?

It's not a choice, but a child

I met a young lady at my practice who has been going through a lot of pain and I had some time to talk to her. She told me a little about herself. Apparently, her previous two marriages ended due to the abuse she suffered. She had some broken bones and a head injury. I felt horrible for her. Then she began to open up and tell me about an abortion she had when she was about 20 years old. While in the exam room preparing for the abortion, she changed her mind, but the physician who was ready to perform the procedure told her "it was too late."

She wept and wept. All I could do was sit there with her, and pray for the right words to say to her. I asked her if she knew the people at Choices Pregnancy Resource Center in Chattanooga, Tennessee. They have a great program to help in the grieving process, no matter how many years after your abortion. She told me that she had met with the people there and they were so kind to her. She made a plaque for the baby. She goes as often as she can to bring toys and other goodies to that plaque. Then she said, "But it will never be enough. I cannot give enough toys to my baby."

I shared a little of Philip's testimony. How I was advised to consider abortion as an option and how there were so many concerns I had for this baby's future. I didn't have a good job, neither did my husband. We had no good health insurance. This would not be a "simple" decision. She replied, "I guess either way, there is pain involved."

Yes, there is pain. But we also have hope, and forgiveness. We prayed together, and I will still keep her in my prayers. I provided contacts for her, because she needs to be in a good support network and not continue in misery alone. Please pray for her.

Maybe you are struggling after the trauma of an abortion, like my friend. There is hope, and with the help and forgiveness of God, there is peace.

Email me and let me know if I can help anyone out there! help@lovewithoutreason.org

Women and the right to....VOTE

There has been a lot of talk in 2012 regarding the "war on women" and the "woman's vote." This is true in regards to the election year, I'm not sure that it is much of an issue otherwise.

Since 1973, **54 million abortions** have occurred in the US alone. You read that right, 54 million babies who were taken from the safety of the womb to be discarded, their life light whisked out. Close to 500 physicians signed a public declaration indicating "Abortion is never necessary to save the life of the mother." (American Life League)

Then, is abortion necessary at all? People, we each have the right to choose our mate. You and I can choose our political party. But don't you dare hide behind the word "choice" when it comes to the life of a baby. You must say it as it is. You either are declaring life or death when it comes to an "unintended pregnancy." Only 8% of abortions fall in the category of source as rape, incest or mother's health. Personal reasons are cited for the 92% remaining, according the National Right to Life website.

It is **PAST** time to stand up for the lives of the children that were destroyed before their time. It is an enemy called Satan who comes to steal, kill, and destroy. Jesus Christ came to give life, and life more abundant. If you don't believe me, take the time to visit the National Memorial for the Unborn in Chattanooga. You will weep when you read the plaques and grave markers of the aborted children whose parents and sometimes grandparents have placed in their honor. How they wish they could turn back the clock. We can't turn it back. However, we can declare today that we will stand up for the right to life of our children. Every child matters. No one is unwanted.

So, yes, there is a war on women. The war to make women think that they have no alternative but death in the case of an unintended pregnancy. The war to make women think that people are trying to dictate what you can or cannot do to your body. The fact is this baby is a new life, separate from yours and mine, that is temporarily housed and sheltered in the womb. And because every child matters, no matter the race, sex, disability or appearance, they deserve life.

Let your voice be heard. There are 54 million voices who will never be heard.

Scribblers

Years ago the young women of our church had the desire to gather together separately from church or family time and just fellowship and build the "sisterhood." The gathering birthed the name, "Scribblers." One young woman was reading a book called Scribbling in the Sand. Another had the idea of "Scribblers" to mean that before anyone learns to write decently and in an orderly fashion, initially they will scribble. So as we were "scribbling" trying to learn what our purpose was in gathering in this fashion, our hope was that God would just take us and use our scribbles to turn into beautiful calligraphy

I said all that to say, I've had the privilege of watching these young women grow from childhood (some from newborns), adolescence, college students, and young married wives and mothers. I can recall babysitting several of them and being involved in their school work. For many, I was their Sunday School teacher. It has been so interesting to see the cycle repeated as they are now the babysitters, mentors and Sunday School teachers for our children. Sowing into the lives of children is never in vain.

The Scribblers have done a variety of projects over the past few years. One favorite fundraiser is the bake sale. A recent bake sale was almost called off by the Chattanooga fire department (ha ha, but we won't get into that). After the bake sale, the Scribblers came together and gave me a card to read.

They had unanimously decided that the funds raised from the bake sale would go towards Love Without Reason®. (This was of course not mentioned to me before I slaved over banana bread and sausage balls!!)

Anyways, I was so touched. I reminded them that the Bible tells us that what we sow, we will most certainly reap. Or in other words, what goes around comes around. When we sow good things, we will surely reap them.

Scribblers International

Scribblers, a young women's ministry in our church that is dedicated to "sisterhood and servant hood" is a work in progress, with plenty of room for improvement; but we're getting there, praise God. When we were in India, specifically in Chitoor, Karnataka, for a mission trip, during the evenings there were open air meetings and during the day Bible studies.

The main speaker for the special meetings was from Sri Lanka, a Pastor Mendis. About 60 people from his church flew to Chitoor and attended the meetings. On Saturday I spoke to a few young women who were from Sri Lanka (I will call them the Scribblers International). The young women were delightful and very sweet and pleasant to talk to. They made me feel very comfortable (Shout out to Vihara, Moughavi, Sister Agnes, and Souganthi).

Well, on Saturday, one of them came to me to talk about her own pain and heartaches in Sri Lanka. Soon a few others joined, and we decided to spend some time in prayer. I remembered that before we left from America, Pastor Abraham encouraged my husband and myself to lay hands and pray for the people. I've never done that before on my own, but I felt that the Lord was telling me to do so. I could not help but weep for the young women who came to pray. They are so dedicated and later I would see that even more so.

I had noticed that a big bus filled with the Sri Lankan believers would arrive almost 2 hours before the evening meetings started. As it turned out, the young women came and talked with me for a little while before the service on Saturday night, before standing together in unison saying "We must go and pray for the meetings, Pastor expects it." I watched all of them go kneel on the hard and rocky earth (open air meeting, remember) and lift their hands and cry out to God. They stayed there on their knees for one hour.

On Sunday night, I could not sit in the crowd, I had to go and join them. It was a powerful time of prayer, I believe. Pastor Mendis has several thousand believers in his church, and it all started with a handful of believers many years ago. He is a prophet, has prophesied about the tsunami and other disasters over the past several years. God even raised a man from the dead through Pastor Mendis' prayer.

It made me think a lot. We can mock our leaders who have done horrible things and are on TV for their sins finding them out. We can disrespect and judge our leaders. We can also complain and point fingers and say there are no results and where is the fruit?! But what if we cried out, in one accord, and prayed for them, what would happen? I learned a lot of things about the Indian culture and more importantly about spiritual warfare and true sacrifice. I heard that some believers were on a schedule waking up every morning 3 a.m. to pray.

The "Scribblers International" do not know what they have done to change some things in my life. I hope that you, too, pray that God would open your eyes to see what needs to change in YOUR life. What needs to be done differently, where is your sacrifice? I promise you, our God is faithful, as I saw with Pastor Mendis and his full blown ministry. But we have to do so in unity, and make sacrifices.

I'll never forget Pastor Sean Teal's message "God will not trust His Kingdom in the hands of prayerless people." May God help you and me to do the same.

"My god on the Earth"

At the July 2012 medical camp in Chennapatna, Karnataka, we met Shivaranjan. He is a handsome 14 year old who at first glance appeared "normal." I thought to myself, "He doesn't have a cleft, he does have two eyes, and two ears." Yet when he tried to speak, I noticed he could barely open his mouth. Ankylosis at his temperomandibular joint and jaw would not allow him to open his mouth. In fact, we learned his parents would ground and liquify his food so he could "drink" it through a straw.

Imagine living 14 years like this. Our team of doctors headed by Dr. Tony Varghese and Dr. Sathish evaluated him and scheduled surgery. Dr. Sathish was able to surgically intervene and successfully complete the surgery and today Shivaranjan can open his mouth fully! He is so thrilled he can eat, chew and talk. He calls Dr.Sathish "my god on earth." The villagers are all in excitement because they know how this young man has lived. A massive life-transforming event has occurred for this young man.

Though the physical man has been healed, we must pray for the inner man to be transformed by the power of Jesus Christ. There are many more young people who are waiting for surgery for a physical transformation. Join our cause in reaching them, and in effect demonstrating the Unconditional Love of God in treating their physical and spiritual needs.

Casting my bread

In the book of Ecclesiastes there is a verse that reads, "Cast your bread upon the waters, for after many days it will return to you." I remember reading that verse so many times as a youth and not understanding the meaning. I learned one interpretation on a recent radio commentary.

The discussion was on the life of Corrie Ten Boom, a brave woman whose house was a safe refuge for the Jews during Hitler's reign. One of Corrie's nephews who was a great speaker, had a speaking engagement in Israel.

Sometime during his stay in Israel, he suffered a massive heart attack. He was cared for by the cardiovascular surgeons in Israel. One of them asked Corrie's nephew if he was in any way related to the "Ten Booms" of Holland. The nephew explained how his aunt had rescued and hid many of the Jewish people from Hitler's regime. The surgeon exclaimed that as a baby, he had been one of those victims rescued by Corrie Ten Boom. How amazing that years later, the same person whose life was saved, now was saving the life of his rescuer.

Talk about goosebumps! The commentary closed by saying we do not know what kind of a difference we are making in the lives of the children, but we do know that whatever bread is cast, it will return to us. We know the verse "reap what you sow."

I used to tell my Sunday School class that their prayers to God are never in vain. Though we may not see an immediate answer, or even the answer we prayed for, we know God hears all prayers. In the same way, I pray that we all would unabashedly sow into the lives of every child that we can. It will never be in vain.

The Stall-Banger

Love Without Reason® has a Facebook page with a place to post what the current status of the author is. For instance, "Susan is.....supposed to be working." One post says Susan is.....ashamed. I have actually done a lot of reflecting and examining of my heart for a few weeks. Let me start from the beginning.

My problem began few weeks ago when I volunteered to help out with my daughter's Fall Party. My daughter Sara is a lot like me in the fact that she has a phobia regarding bathrooms. She despises any other bathroom, other than her own in her home. You can imagine my concern over her "holding it" for 8 or more hours during school. Well, she finally has overcome the fear, and uses the school restroom now without difficulty. She was excited and wanted to show off to me. (This is the first time I have actually been able to do anything at her school due to my work schedule).

I hate school restrooms! Walking in there with her brought all sorts of bad memories from my school days. Ugh! The toilet paper, the smells, that horrible stringy soap, the crowded stalls! To top it off, after Sara was settled in her stall, another young girl banged on her door stating that she had to go "right now!" I was like, you have to wait!!!

Well, we finally made our exit, when I heard this voice behind me ask, "Can you tie my shoe?" (It was the stall-banger). All I could envision was dirty shoelaces, dirty floors, snotty-nosed kids, and bacteria. I walked on, and heard the question two more times before I returned Sara to her classroom.

Well, I heard that question and saw that little girl in my mind all the way home. I was convicted. I used to wonder what people meant when they said "think outside the box, or get out of your comfort zone." I thought I already do this!!! Now, I think one meaning may be, put aside the things that hinder or prevent you from moving forward to your goal.

I was so blinded by the fear (of any illness), environment (strange restroom and unfamiliar people), that I could not hear a child asking for help. I berated myself... I mean how can I help my LWR babies if I can't answer a call to tie a shoe? May God help me.

Good in Hollywood

My daughter Sara has discovered the movie, "Prince of Egypt." She now loves the story of Moses, and Philip enjoys singing all the songs in the movie. I've now seen the movie 2 or 3 times. I love the opening song, "Deliver us." It's a powerful song. Well, I was sitting there with the kids watching the movie and just thought about the oppressor of the Israelites, that is Egypt. The Egyptians had enslaved and oppressed the Israelites. The king of Egypt wanted to ensure that an army would not be raised by the growing generation of Israeli young men.

Therefore, he ordered all baby boys to be killed. Moses, the Israelite who should have been killed with the other babies, was rescued by the royal family of Egypt, and raised in the palace of the King of Egypt. He does not know his true origin. After he learns he is not an Egyptian, other slaves mock him and ask why has he come to "deliver" the Israelites to the Promised Land and how could he not have known that his own people were slaves. In the movie, Moses responds, "I did not see, because I did not wish to see."

It was an eye-opening movie, especially as I tried to put in perspective with the crime of human trafficking. I thought of the testimony of fifteen year old Elizabeth (name changed, from the International Justice Mission). She was sold to a brothel by her aunt. After months of torture, rape, neglect, she was rescued by the workers of IJM. You and I both could walk away from her story and say I do not want to see or believe this, so I'll close my eyes to it. Friend, is that what you want to do? I some nights cannot sleep, because I hear that cry of the children "Deliver us!" I pray that you will also hear and answer that call. Please pray for us as we desire to raise the awareness of sex trafficking, to deliver and restore the lives of these victims.

Innocence of Children

I do not have a green thumb, (it's brown actually, ha ha). However, I have wanted to plant pansies for several years, and have been unable to do so for one reason or another. I just wanted to see if they would really live after being planted during the winter season.

One December I finally had the opportunity to buy pansies, and to plant them. I asked the clerks at the nursery "I heard it's still not too late to plant pansies, right?" They affirmed everything, and tried to talk me through on how to plant them.

Well, after planting them, we had a horrible freeze for about 2 weeks in January. My youngest baby, Caleb, came to me after looking at the pansies I had planted. He had tears in his eyes and pointed at the green shrubs and said "Where's the flowers, mommy?" He made me want to cry. I felt horrible for him. He remembered seeing the flowers, and now they were gone, leaving only the green leaves.

The precious children are so innocent, aren't they? They do not have a clue. They are so trusting, never doubting a word. I think this is all the more reason that we should do everything to protect them.

From conception onwards, fight to protect the lives of the innocent. If no one stands up for the unprotected and innocent babes, then what will happen to our future generation? I urge you readers to take a stand for the lives of our children. We must protect our future and our posterity. Pray for the children, and ask God what you can do to work and speak and transform the lives our innocent children.

The power of prayer

When we were expecting our daughter Sara, it was our prayer that we would have a girl, and she would be a help and a champion for Philip. We were so concerned about the reaction of the world to Philip and his appearance, and for that reason we prayed for a sibling who would stand with and support him.

Sara has been just that to Philip. Of course they still get into their occasional spats and the 'he said, she said' arguments. But I've seen her get in between Philip and children twice her size that are making fun of Philip. Once we were taking family pictures in a studio, and I believe she was four years old. Other kids waiting to take pictures stared and laughed at Philip. She was so upset, yet she asked Philip if she could go and 'hurt that boy.' That's my girl!!!

I guess what I never expected is that Sara would take that 'prayer' over her life, and let it go outside of Philip. In first grade, there was another classmate with her who had Down's syndrome. Though she was in the classroom, this little girl would not listen to the teacher always, and may have sometimes been disruptive.

Apparently, Sara would encourage her to get on the right path. She would come and hug her or pat her on the shoulder to love on her even though this little girl did not understand or know to respond back to Sara's kindness. I never knew she was doing this until recently. The mother of that little girl came to us and asked if Sara would give her a hug. Sara was shy with the mom, but she did. Mom went on to tell us what Sara had done for her daughter. She had been so encouraged, because so many others could not look past her daughter's differences.

Tears just came to my eyes. My little girl already has a testimony. What power there is in prayer! How faithful my God is to me! Just as the Word says, He knows our thoughts afar off. Many things may not go the way I want them to, but I know that He hears every prayer. He knows. And He is in control.

Caleb's testimony

As we were gathered for family prayer, our three children discussed the persecution of believers in other parts of the world. Philip said, "I don't want to go to China, because they might persecute and kill me." His younger brother, Caleb, boldly countered, "I will go to China. Even if they put me in prison, God will send an earthquake to release me from prison." We talked a little about evangelization and the protection of God.

We asked Caleb what exactly he would share while in other countries. He responded, "I'll share my testimony. And, Mom, I didn't have any surgeries like Philip, did I?"

We all had a good laugh. Caleb did not have any surgeries. However, as an infant, he suffered with extreme eczema on his face and scalp. His itching and oozing and crusting on his face and scalp grieved us. We went through literally thirty different medications and several specialists. We sanitized the house and everyone's clothing and linen. It was a massive effort, and nothing seemed to help Caleb. Deliverance and healing came in the presence of God. With much prayer and intercession, we began to see changes in Caleb's skin.

As a child he began to suffer with seasonal allergies, with cough, congestion, nasal drainage and itchy eyes. This continued for many years, till one day, in the presence of the Lord, he was healed. We saw complete deliverance for our son. His allergies stopped bothering him and he was set free.

Recently, the kids dressed up in different Bible character costumes for a program at church. Philip wanted to be King David, Sara wanted to be Abraham's wife Sarah, but Caleb insisted that he was going to dress as Caleb. As the kids talked about the merits of each character, Caleb said "I like Caleb because the Bible does not tell us that Caleb committed any sin, like King David did. So I want to be Caleb!" I must say that was pretty deep for a seven year old.

I pray that our little Caleb does one day become like the strong and mighty warrior in the scriptures that he is named after and be a voice for Jesus Christ to all nations.

About the Author

Susan Mathews is the co-founder of Love Without Reason®, a United States nonprofit organization based in Chattanooga, Tennessee.

Susan is a Family Nurse Practitioner who has worked in the health care industry for over 15 years. She and her husband of 15 years, Santhosh Mathews, have three children, Philip, Sara and Caleb and live in Chattanooga, TN. Susan and Santhosh also serve as the youth ministers at the Chattanooga Christian Assembly.

As a result of their personal experiences with their son Philip Mathews, who was born with Goldenhar's syndrome, Susan and Santhosh founded Love Without Reason® to raise awareness for those who are lured into the evils of sex trafficking and beggary and to help people born with craniofacial deformities by providing holistic care and surgical intervention.

Email Susan at *info@lovewithoutreason*.**org** and let us know if this book has touched your life. Send us your testimonies to be included in our next book about your experiences with a special needs child. Philip, Susan and Santhosh Mathews are available for speaking engagements upon request.

Support the cause of Love Without Reason by sending your donations to P.O. Box 21009, Chattanooga TN 37424. Make your checks payable to "**Love Without Reason**." For more information on please visit http://www.lovewithoutreason.org.

"Because Every Child Matters"